THE FOOT GUARDS REGIMENTS

1880-1914

A pictorial album

compiled by

A. H. Bowling

ALMARK PUBLISHING CO. LTD., LONDON

First published—January 1972

ISBN 0 85524 052 0 (hard cover edition)
ISBN 0 85524 053 9 (paper covered edition)

By the same Author:
BRITISH INFANTRY REGIMENTS, 1660-1914
SCOTTISH REGIMENTS AND UNIFORMS, 1660-1914
INDIAN CAVALRY REGIMENTS, 1880-1914

Printed in Great Britain by
Vale Press Ltd., Mitcham, Surrey CR4 4HR
for the publishers, Almark Publishing Co. Ltd.
270 Burlington Road, New Malden,
Surrey, KT3 4NL,
England.

The Regiments of Foot Guards, 1880-1914

THE pictures in this book have been selected to illustrate the dress worn by the foot regiments of the Brigade of Guards during the period prior to the First World War. During this period many illustrations were appearing in the weekly periodicals whereby much knowledge of uniform detail can be obtained. The best references are the *Army and Navy Gazette, The Regiment,* and the *Illustrated London News.* Also, towards the end of the period a noted photographer, Mrs. Albert Broom, was taking many photographs of the Guards regiments stationed in the London area. To many people the regiments of Foot Guards are only associated with their duties at the Royal palaces but besides these guards they also furnished the Tower of London guard, the Bank of England picquet and detachments for the Central London Recruiting Depot and the Magazine in Hyde Park.

The first regiment of the Brigade, the Grenadier Guards, dates from 1656 when a unit known as Wentworth's Regiment was formed in the Netherlands. This was part of a force formed by the exiled monarch Charles II and financed by the King of Spain. By custom, regiments at this time were referred to by the Colonel's name, the actual title of this regiment being 'His Majestie's Regiment of Guards'. On the restoration of the monarchy the regiment took precedence over other regiments and in 1685 became the 1st Regiment of Foot Guards. The battle honours of the Grenadier Guards start with 'Tangier 1680' and prior to the 1914-18 war ended with 'South Africa 1899-1902', between these dates are the honours for the Marlborough campaigns, the long war against Napoleon's armies ending with the honour 'Waterloo' and later honours for the Crimea and Egyptian wars. Of interest is the fact that the title Grenadier was granted in 1815 when the regiment received the title 'The 1st or Grenadier Regiment of Foot Guards', this being a compliment for the part that the regiment had played at Waterloo when they defeated the famous grenadier battalions of Napoleon's Old Guard. On receiving the title 'Grenadier' the regiment wore the fur cap in all battalions, a distinction which previously had applied only to the grenadier companies. The dress distinctions of the regiment are the white plume worn on the left side of the bearskin cap, a bursting grenade badge, buttons evenly spaced and a red band on the forage cap. These distinctions can still be

3

The guardsman and Colour Sergeant are wearing the peakless Broderick cap issued to the army between 1902 and 1905. The Sergeant's tunic differs from the first class tunic by having no gold lace on the collar or around the cuffs. The badge above his right cuff is for a qualified musketry instructor. The drummer and corporal are in full dress. The corporal's stripes are of white worsted and above his left cuff is the badge for musketry proficiency.

seen in the present day uniform.

The second regiment of the Brigade, the Coldstream Guards, were raised in 1650 as 'Monck's Regiment', part of Cromwell's New Model Army. Shortly before the Restoration, Monck's forces met at Coldstream in Berwickshire and marched to London as part of Monck's plan to support Charles II. After Charles' arrival in London most of the Parliamentary forces were disbanded but Monck's regiment was only formally discharged as it was immediately re-embodied. The title 'Coldstream Regiment of Foot Guards' was granted in 1670 after Monck's death, this title remaining until 1817 when the regiment assumed the present title 'Coldstream Guards'. The badge of the regiment is the star of the Order of the Garter and the dress distinctions include the tunic buttons worn in pairs, the red plume on the right side of the bearskin cap, and the forage cap with a white band. The battle honours of the regiment are very similar to those of the Grenadier Guards starting with 'Tangier 1680' and ending pre-1914 with 'South Africa 1899-1902'. The 2nd Battalion were present at Waterloo.

The regiment of 'Scotch Guards' placed on the establishment in 1661 was in fact a revival of units which served between 1639 and 1651. Various titles of the regiment over the years included from 1661 to 1712 'The Scotch Guards', 1712 to 1813, '3rd Foot Guards', 1831 to 1877 'Scots Fusilier Guards' and from 1877 to date 'Scots Guards'. The badge of the regiment is the star of the Order of the Thistle, the collar badge being a thistle. The regiment have no plume on the bearskin cap, and the buttons are worn in threes, a diced band being worn on the forage cap. The battle honours are in line with those of the previous regiments but starting with 'Namur 1695'.

The Irish Guards were raised in April 1900. This was Her Majesty Queen Victoria's idea as a means of honouring the South African War services of the Irish regiments. The first colonel was, appropriately enough, Field Marshal Lord Roberts, VC. A St Patrick's blue plume was worn on the right side of the bearskin cap, the tunic had buttons grouped in fours and bore a shamrock collar badge. The forage cap had a green band.

In 1914 the Grenadier Guards had three battalions stationed at Warley, Chelsea, and Wellington Barracks respectively. The three battalions of the Coldstream Guards were at Aldershot, Chelsea, and Windsor. The Scots Guards had two battalions stationed at Aldershot and the Tower of London respectively and the single battalion of Irish Guards was stationed at Wellington Barracks.

All illustrations in this book are from the author's personal collection. Sources include contemporary magazines of the period, miscellaneous prints, plus private photographs and popular postcards. The photographs reproduced in colour were black and white originals tinted in the appropriate colours and sold in this form. Colour photography as such was, of course, not a commercial proposition in the period covered by this book although it is of interest to note that some colour cine film of military subjects, notably the Royal Durbar in India in 1911, existed at this time. This again, though, was reproduced by a rudimentary tinting process and was not a true colour film in the modern sense. The last two pictures in the book are courtesy the Imperial War Museum.

A drummer and two privates of the Grenadier Guards in Egypt on active service in 1882. The privates have the Martini-Henry rifle and wear the valise equipment of 1866. Note the regimental badge on the oilskin-covered valise and the flat field service cap strapped up with the rolled greatcoat. The serge frock was scarlet with plain dark blue collar and cuffs and no piping. Trousers were dark blue with narrow red stripe; gaiters were black leather, helmet and accoutrements white.

A battalion transport wagon of the Brigade of Guards, the wagon appears to be of the type 'Wagon, General Service, Mark IV'. The horses pulling the wagon are wearing the wheel set breast pole draught harness while the horse of the guardsman in front has lead set harness. Note that the men are wearing Bedford cord breeches and puttees.

The Grenadier Guards

ABOVE: A battalion parade for annual inspection, the first man in the front rank is a Colour-Sergeant acting as marker and he is holding a company colour. BELOW: The new guard presenting arms to the colour before marching from Wellington Barracks to Buckingham Palace for the Guard Mounting ceremony.

ABOVE: A Company Sergeant-Major waiting before handing the King's Colour to the Ensign. The sergeants in khaki service dress attend the inspection for the purpose of taking down reports.

The 1st Battalion, Grenadier Guards, 1896. To the left of the Colours, a corporal drummer, drum-major and drummer, to the right the adjutant in frock coat and the battalion commanding officer. The company badge on the Regimental Colour (right) is that of the 20th company, the head of King Charles II in the branches of a green oak tree.

LEFT: A Regimental Sergeant-Major, his dress distinctions being the first class tunic with gold lace on collar and cuffs and the large embroidered Royal Arms on the right arm above the elbow. RIGHT: A guardsman in marching order; he is wearing Slade-Wallace equipment and is armed with the Lee-Metford rifle, his pillbox cap is dark blue with a red band. At this time the rank of Private was still used in the Guards.

ABOVE: Pioneers were among the first men in the army to be classed as tradesmen and the trade badge of a grenade above crossed axes is worn on the right upper arm. LEFT: Holding spades and pick-axes, the Pioneers did not carry rifles. The pouches on the waistbelt were replaced by frogs to enable various tools to be carried. The wearing of beards was confirmed by a General Order of November 18, 1856.

A Drum-Major in State Clothing. The badge of the Grenadier Guards is much in evidence in this picture being borne on the embroidered sash and as clips to fasten the crimson sash, the garters fastened below the knee were covered with gold lace.

The single spacing of the Grenadier Guards buttons is clearly shown by the lacing on this drummer's tunic, the white plume worn on the left side of the bearskin cap does not show from the front as it is brushed into the bearskin. The drum appears to be a practice drum as there is no sign of ornamentation on the front.

A sergeant standing at 'order arms'. The ranks from Sergeant to Regimental Sergeant-Major wear a crimson sash over the right shoulder. The sergeant's tunic known as 'sergeants quality' has gold lace only on the cuff slashes, back of skirt, and gold lace chevrons. Originally sergeants and corporals were the only NCOs in infantry regiments, sergeant-majors ranking as NCOs being introduced during the first part of the 18th century.

Before the South African War the Guards carried out field exercises wearing full dress uniforms and appeared much as they would at a Guard Mounting parade, the difference being that on exercises the haversack and water bottle were carried and black gaiters were worn. The valise was not always carried. The inverted chevron is a service stripe denoting 3 years' service.

The officers of the 3rd Battalion, Grenadier Guards, 1897. Most of the officers are wearing the dark blue undress frock coat. This form of dress with the coat braided in black mohair and with black tracing cord on the collar and cuffs plus the addition of the crimson sash and white sword belt was in fact an exceptionally smart dress. The three officers wearing riding boots are the Adjutant, 2nd in Command and the Officer Commanding. The officers standing in the back row who are wearing flat forage caps are in the red frock or jacket, this had a blue collar, cuffs and shoulder straps.

A drummer of the Grenadier Guards, 1896. This picture illustrates the drummer's sword; the hilt was brass and the scabbard was black leather with brass mountings.

The senior NCOs of the 1st Bn, Grenadier Guards about 1897. Lance-Sergeants are in the back two rows, sergeants in the middle two rows, and drill colour, and quartermaster sergeants in the front two rows. The staff sergeants, 1st class and quartermaster sergeants have four chevrons. In the front row note the Drum-Major (right). Quartermaster, battalion second-in-command, Lieut-Colonel commanding, and RSM (fourth to eighth from right respectively).

Grenadier Guards on summer exercises about 1898. The sergeant holding the Lee-Metford rifle above his head is giving the field signal ENEMY IN SIGHT this was indicated by the rifle being raised and lowered frequently. Both the Lance Sergeant and private are wearing the very practical field service cap (or side cap) which was then in vogue for drills, fatigues, and active service. It was dark blue with red piping and facings for the Grenadiers.

The Coldstream Guards

A scene at annual camp. The Adjutants of the Grenadier and Coldstream Guards are here seen lining up the tent poles. Interesting features of this picture are the small differences shown in dress and horse furniture; while the Grenadier Adjutant is wearing white gloves the Coldstream Adjutant appears to be wearing brown. Also note the devices on the black leather sabretasche, an article abolished in 1902: the Imperial Cypher surmounted by a crown for the Grenadiers and the Garter Star for the Coldstream. Most interesting perhaps is the Garter Star on the bit of the Coldstream Guards officer's horse.

ABOVE: Men in full marching order resting while on a route march, 1897. The Adjutant is speaking to a company officer. Both officers are carrying haversacks slung over the right shoulder. Among the men can be seen two lance sergeants and a corporal. To the right can be seen the entrenching tool that could be attached to the Slade-Wallace equipment that the men are wearing. The Garter Star badge worn on the valise can be seen on the man in the foreground.

OPPOSITE: A Grenadier guardsman in marching order, 1888. The equipment was the 1882 pattern. This consisted of waist belt, pouches and straps of white buff leather, the black valise being worn low on the back. The mess tins in a black waterproof cover were placed on top of the valise. The haversack strap was worn over the right shoulder and the water bottle strap over the left shoulder. This can be seen on the figure in the background. The rifle was the Martini-Henry of 1871. Note the crossed rifles of the musketry proficiency badge.

LEFT: A guardsman at the end of his recruit training and ready to take his place in the ranks of the battalion, in full marching order with forage cap. RIGHT: The same order of dress but the forage cap is here replaced by the bearskin cap. The Garter Star was worn on the collar and shoulder straps, and also on the valise. The rifle is the Lee-Metford.

LEFT: The Lieutenant-Colonel commanding 1st Coldstream Guards, in the dark blue frock coat on which all the braid was black. A crimson sash was worn over the left shoulder and the white sword belt round the waist. RIGHT: The Lieutenant-Colonel commanding 2nd Coldstream Guards. These two photographs of the left and right side show how the sword was carried by Field Officers. The forage cap was dark blue with a black band.

A bugler of the Mounted Infantry detachment, Grenadier Guards. The main reason for the formation of the mounted infantry was to have speed of movement and concentration of fire power. Although officially approved in 1888, mounted infantry had been used as early as 1875 but their most important services were during the South African War. After this war they gradually faded out and by 1914 had almost ceased to exist. The Brigade of Guards sent composite companies to South Africa. The first kit was the infantry uniform with corduroy trousers, these being replaced by breeches and puttees. The standard infantry rifle and bayonet was used and the horse furniture was usually of the regulation cavalry type. Note the bandolier of ammunition. This man is wearing the Germanic style 'Broderick cap' a type of forage cap introduced in 1905 and named after the then Minister of War.

Coldstream Guards 1895. The equipment worn is the Slade-Wallace 1888 pattern, the valise being worn high on the back. The haversack strap is worn over the right shoulder, and the water bottle strap over the left shoulder. The frog for the entrenching tool was attached to the waist belt. The rifle is the Lee-Metford 1887 which replaced the Martini-Henry. Note how the rifle was carried at the slope, a style changed when magazine rifles made their appearance.

ABOVE: Guard Mounting at the Tower; the old and new guard exchanging compliments. The barracks at the Tower of London were normally occupied by a battalion of one of the Guards regiments, but although the Guards furnish the Tower Guard nowadays only a small detachment from the battalion furnishing the guards for the Royal Palaces in London is called on for this duty. The notable feature of this duty is the nightly escort for the Keys, this ceremony begins at 9.50 p.m. when an escort of a sergeant, drummer and two guardsmen accompany the Chief Warder on his rounds and ends with a challenge by the sentry on the Jewel House 'Halt! who comes there,' on the reply 'The Keys' the sentry asks 'Whose keys?' and receives the reply 'Queen Elizabeth's Keys'. The sentry then gives 'Pass Queen Elizabeth's Keys' and the Chief Warder replies 'God preserve Queen Elizabeth' and all present answer 'Amen'.

RIGHT: The State Colour of the Coldstream Guards is one of two presented to the regiment by King William IV. Crimson with a gold fringe and with crimson and gold tassels, the colour bears in the centre the Star of the Order of the Garter surrounded by a Union wreath with the Imperial Crown above. In each corner is a silver Sphinx between two gold branches of laurel. The first of the two colours bears six battle honours, the second nine. The Ensign in full dress is wearing the special gold laced sash used when this colour is carried. The State Colour is only carried by a Guard of Honour on State occasions when the Sovereign is present. The officer on the left of the picture is the Adjutant. This picture dates from about 1899.

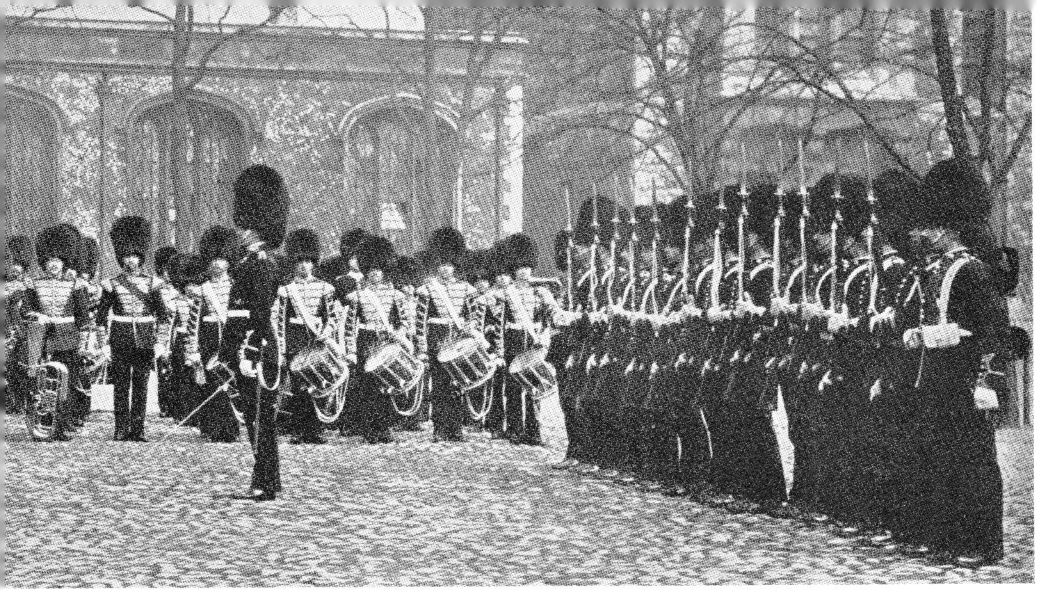

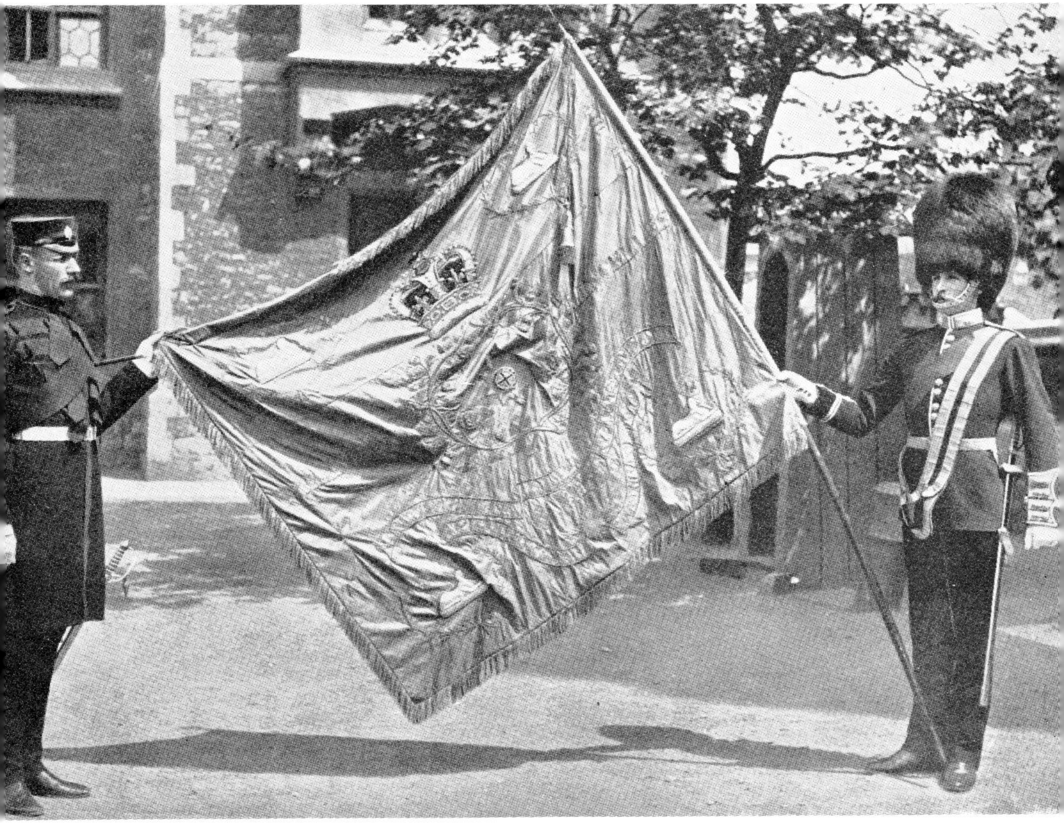

0,175

The Coldstream Guards, 1905. The Regimental Sergeant-Major carrying the King's Colour escorted by two guardsmen. In the Brigade of Guards the Crimson colour was the King's (or Queen's) Colour and the Union the Regimental Colour. In the Line Infantry this is reversed, the Union being the King's Colour, the coloured being the Regimental. The earliest record of the Coldstream Guards colours is given in an account of a review of General Monck's Regiment in 1669 when the standard was green with a red cross and six white balls. At this time the facings were green, being changed to blue in 1685. In 1696 the Colonel's Colour was crimson and the Star of the Order of the Garter was placed on the Lieutenant-Colonel's and Major's Colours for the first time. Crimson for the Queen's colour has been used continually since 1696. The medals worn by the escort are for the South African War: This is reproduced from a postcard of the period.

The State Clothing for the Drum-Majors of the Foot Guards. The State Clothing has remained almost the same since the time of Charles II. Contemporary drawings of the Coronation of James II, 1688, show musicians of the Foot Guards wearing crimson coats, faced with blue and heavily laced with gold. This was in fact the Royal Livery and was worn by Court musicians as well as the Household troops. An account of the clothing for the Grenadier Guards Drum-Major in 1713 quotes this coat with the embroidered cypher and crown of Queen Anne on the front and back, also the crimson gold fringed scarf worn round the waist. The embroidered sash bore regimental badges and scrolls bearing the regimental battle honours. This picture dates from 1905.

This print published in 1895 shows a drummer, lieutenant, and guards-man in full dress, this was the dress and equipment worn on full dress parades such as Guard Mounting. On State occasions the officers' sash was crimson and gold and the waist belt and sword slings were gold laced, the sword knot being gold also. The officers' trousers had a 2 in. wide scarlet stripe but at Levees they wore trousers with a $1\frac{1}{2}$ in. wide gold stripe down the side seams.

OPPOSITE: The seated figure is the Pioneer Sergeant. His tunic is of sergeants' quality with no lace on the collar or round the cuffs. His badge of rank worn on the right arm consists of three gold chevrons with crossed axes and a small grenade above. A General Order of 1856 allowed for one pioneer per company in each regiment. The tools carried by the pioneers included a sawbacked sword, pickaxe, billhooks and shovels. The same order stated that gauntlets and aprons had ceased to be part of a pioneer's equipment. Behind is the Regimental Sergeant Major flanked by two Drill Sergeants. The Colour Badge on the Regimental Drill Ser-geants' chevrons was a crimson flag with the Garter Star and Sphinx badges surmounted by a crown and crossed swords beneath the flag.

Scots Guards, Regimental Sergeant-Major, 1905; the senior Warrant Officer in the regiment. In the Brigade of Guards the large size Royal Arms worn on the right arm above the elbow denoted this rank. In full dress parade order the black bearskin cap, without plume for Scots Guards, would be worn. His medals are the Queen's and King's South African War medals, a campaign for which the regiment received the battle honour 'South Africa 1899-1902'. The rank of Sergeant-Major appears to have been introduced early in the 18th century as before this the only NCOs were Sergeants and Corporals.

Scots Guards, Drummer 1905. The main feature of the drummer's uniform was the lacing on the front of the tunic and on the arms and back seams, the lace being white with a blue fleur-de-lys pattern. The fleur-de-lys was once part of the Royal Coat of Arms. The early history of drummers indicates that they were men of considerable importance within a regiment. During the reign of Queen Elizabeth I a writer states that drummers were required to speak foreign languages as they were often sent to parley with the enemy and to redeem and conduct prisoners; also they were required not to disclose any secrets that they knew.

LEFT: The lace on the tunics for drummers and fifers of the Brigade of Guards is placed on the front of the tunic according to the regimental button grouping. This bugler is wearing black gaiters and carries the short drummer's sword, c. 1899. RIGHT: A Regimental Drill Sergeant of 1895, complete with pace stick and carrying the staff sergeants' pattern sword in a black leather scabbard with gilt mountings. His cap is dark blue with a band of gold lace and gold passing braid on the peak.

ABOVE: For ranks below that of officer there were three types of tunics, first class, sergeants', and rank and file qualities. The first class was worn by Warrant Officers, but there were certain ranks which had a mixture of first class and sergeant's quality tunics. The photographs taken in 1913 show an Orderly Room Sergeant (left) wearing a sergeant's tunic laced as for Warrant Officers but with only one band of lace round each cuff. He is accompanied by two Staff Sergeants and a Battalion Drill Sergeant. BELOW. The Warrant Officer on the right is a Regimental Quartermaster Sergeant, he wears a first class tunic with a four bar chevron surmounted by a star on the right arm, when full dress was reintroduced after the 1914-18 War his badge became that of a Warrant Officer, Class II, a Crown within a Wreath of Laurel above the cuff.

The Scots Guards, Piper, Guardsman and Officer, 1896. Pipers appear to have accompanied the Scots Guards since their formation. Although not on the establishment a book of the period states 'any captain may keep a piper, and maintain him too, for no pay is allowed him'. The first official record of a piper on the establishment is in 1704 when a Highland Company was formed, but captains of the other companies still had to provide pipers at their own expense. Unofficially the first Pipe Major was appointed in 1853 and it was not until 1856 that approval was granted for one Pipe Major and five pipers for each battalion being added to the establishment. For the officers and guardsmen the uniform has changed very little since 1857. During the Crimean War the coatee was abolished and a double-breasted tunic introduced; this being soon changed to the single breasted pattern shown here.

A drummer in the khaki clothing worn by the regiment when on service during the South African War; the clothing was of a light colour with brass buttons and the khaki helmet cover is clearly shown. The drums of the Coldstream Guards were painted dark blue and bore the Royal Coat of Arms and regimental devices, the drum rims were white edged red with a central worm of blue. The drum cover was made of blue and white striped ticken. It was carried rolled up and taped to the side of the drum. This dress was known as 'Foreign Service Uniform'.

2nd COLDSTREAM GUARDS.

ABOVE: The band playing before marching from Chelsea Barracks at the head of the new guard. The bandsmen's tunics were basically the same as for the guardsmen but with the addition of gold lace on the front, cuff slash, tunic skirt and wings, while the band sergeants had additional lace on the collar and round the cuffs and carried swords in steel scabbards.
BELOW: Bandsmen preparing for a rehearsal. The flat forage cap was dark blue with a white band. This was the uniform worn when playing in London's Royal parks during the summer season where the bands of the Guards regiments enjoyed great popularity at their afternoon and evening concerts.

OPPOSITE: The Drum Major wears a first class tunic with additional gold lace on the front, sleeves and back seams. His badge of rank is the four bar chevron worn point upwards above the right cuff and the crimson sash worn by sergeants and warrant officers. The embroidered sash worn over the left shoulder is dark blue laced with gold and is ornamented with the Imperial Crown, the regimental badge and a Silver Sphinx. Surrounding these badges are scrolls containing the regimental battle honours, the staff head also bears the Garter badge and Sphinx.

This fifer shows how the lace on the sleeves is worn and how the lace is placed in pairs on the front of the tunic. The fife case is carried on the right side of the waist belt and the bugle cords pass under the right shoulder strap.

A Lance-Sergeant, Corporal and drummers of the Corps of Drums of the Coldstream Guards in 1913. The rank chevron of the NCOs, worn on the right arm, were white as were the service chevrons worn above the left cuff. These chevrons, worn by ranks below Lance-Sergeant on the drummer's tunic, were worn point downwards whereas for guardsmen they were worn point upwards.

The Adjutant, Drum Major and drummers of the 1st Battalion, Coldstream Guards, 1898. The drum and fife were among the earliest instruments of military music, the fife being the name given to the B flat flute. The combination of drum and fife in Europe was copied from the armies of the old Turkish Empire and reached England in the early part of the 16th century.

Among the many and varied tasks undertaken by soldiers this exercise in bridge building carried out under the guidance of the Pioneer Sergeant is an example, two sergeants and the two buglers standing on the ramp wear their white drill jackets while the rest of the men are in shirt sleeve order. The shirt was grey. The company colour is that of the 15th Company, the Crown of Charlemagne all proper on a Union flag.

The colours of the 1st Battalion, 1899. Since 1868, Queen's Regulations give the measurements for the colours as being 3 feet 9 inches wide and 3 feet deep, exclusive of fringe, the pike including the Royal Crest being 8 feet 7½ inches from 1898. The Queen's Colour to the left of the picture was crimson and bore a central device of the Star of the Order of the Garter surmounted by an Imperial Crown, below the Star a Sphinx. This colour also bore scrolls showing the regimental battle honours. The Regimental Colour to the right is the Union also bearing the Crown, Sphinx and battle honours but with a central device of a company badge. The drums in the foreground are decorated with the Royal Coat of Arms with a background of draped colours, the Regimental badges and battle honours. The central figure is the Regimental Sergeant Major and the colours are flanked by two guardsmen in guard order armed with the Lee-Metford rifle.

Sergeants of the Coldstream Guards, 1897. The variety of dress worn by Sergeants and Warrant Officers is shown among the standing figures, the Lance Sergeants having white chevrons, no crimson sash and a white band round the forage cap. The sergeants have gold chevrons, a crimson sash and a gold band round the forage cap. In the front row seated wearing peaked forage caps are the Warrant Officers. The sergeant at the end of the row is an Armourer Sergeant of the Army Ordnance Corps.

The commanding officer and officers of the 2nd Battalion in 1897. They are all wearing the undress uniform, a dark blue forage cap with a black band and the dark blue frock coat which was ornamented with black mohair braid. They have white sword belts and crimson sashes. The blue cloth trousers had a 2 inch wide scarlet stripe. Amongst the seated officers next to the Colonel is a General Officer wearing a cocked hat and two seats away also wearing a cocked hat is a senior member of the General's staff. The General is possibly the Major-General commanding the Household Brigade.

The officers of the 1st Battalion, Coldstream Guards shortly before the South African War. Most of the officers are wearing full dress with black gaiters but three officers in the group are wearing the undress frock. In the Dress Regulations jackets worn in undress are always described under the term frock. For the three regiments of Guards at this time both a red and a blue frock are described, the red frock having a blue collar and blue shoulder straps, the other being all blue. For all regiments there were six buttons down the front, these being spaced singly for the Grenadiers, in pairs for the Coldstream, and in threes for the Scots Guards. The officer standing in the doorway is wearing a folding field cap. The two officers with cocked hats are a Major General and a Colonel on the Staff.

40

The Scots Guards

The Drum Major with drummers and fifers. The three types of drums used can be seen. The corporal on the left has a side drum. The drummer to the right has a tenor drum while in the centre is the bass drum. The three figures to the left are wearing black gaiters and carrying haversacks and water bottles. Although the drummers in this picture do not wear leg aprons the marks left by the pipeclay can be clearly seen on all the tunics.

This scene, so typical of tented camps during manoeuvres, shows men of the Scots Guards cleaning equipment. Among the many items to be cleaned can be seen straps and pouches and the harness for the water bottle. On the blanket in the foreground can be seen a rolled cape and a valise among other items of equipment. The men in their grey shirts and forage caps show a side of army life that is so essential to the smartness of the soldier in parade dress. An interesting figure is the soldier sitting on the extreme right of the picture. He is a piper wearing tartan trews; these were made up from old kilts and were worn in camp or barracks when the piper was off duty. They were not official issue.

A corporal with drummers and buglers. The contrast in their appearance with that of the drummers in camp is clearly shown. This photograph was probably among the last to be taken showing the drummer's sword being worn, as this item was declared obsolete in 1905 although bandsmen of the Guards regiments still retained their special pattern swords which were slightly more elaborate than those of the drummers.

A drummer, 1913. This picture shows very clearly the arrangement of lace and buttons on the tunic, also the fringes on the collar and wings. The way that the lace is placed on the tunics has hardly varied since the introduction of the coattee at the beginning of the 19th Century.

44

ABOVE: The signallers of the 1st Battalion, Scots Guards in 1897. The Lance Sergeant in charge wore his appointment badge of crossed flags above the rank chevrons on the right arm. For the other signallers the proficiency badge was worn above the left cuff. The man on the right has below his signal badge a musketry proficiency badge and two service chevrons. Among the equipment shown can be seen the heliographs used for daylight signalling when the mirror could reflect the sun's light, lanterns for night use and flags, for short distances during daylight. Besides being proficient with these signalling methods the first requirement was to learn and pass in Morse Code.

OPPOSITE PAGE, FAR LEFT: A guardsman in marching order, 1897. The pillbox cap was of blue cloth with a regimental pattern diced band. The tunic of the type known as 'rank and file' had white braid on the cuff slashes and on the back of the skirt. The buttons of the Scots Guards have been grouped in threes since 1775.

OPPOSITE RIGHT: Scots Guards 1882. A guardsman in guard order wearing the valise equipment and armed with the Martini-Henry rifle 1871 pattern, the calibre of this rifle was 0·450 in., and was a breech loading weapon sighted up to 1,000 yards. This rifle was issued to the Scots Guards in October 1874 and was replaced by a magazine rifle in 1890.

*A Lieutenant in undress frock coat and a 2nd Lieutenant in full dress,
1895. From 1880 to 1904 2nd Lieutenants did not wear a rank star on
the shoulder straps. Note that the crimson sash is worn on the opposite
shoulder to the senior NCO's sash.*

ABOVE: The Pipe Major, Corporal Pipers and pipers, of the 1st Bn. Scots Guards. A photograph taken at Wellington Barracks in 1913. BELOW: Pipe Major Frazer and two pipers of the 1st Battalion 1897. The Pipe Major's banner was crimson, but all other pipers carried blue banners.

The Pipe Major of the 1st Battalion 1897. His doublet is dark blue with silver braid and buttons. His rank is shown by the silver crown above four silver chevrons worn on the right arm above the gauntlet cuff. The tartan and pipe streamers were Royal Stuart as were the rosettes placed above and below the kilt pin.

A piper in 1913; this was the full dress for pipers until 1914 and from 1920 to 1928 in which year King George V granted permission for the pipers of the Scots Guards to wear the feather bonnet with a blue over red hackle plume on the left side, as is still worn today.

BELOW: A Drum Major wearing full dress but without the embroidered sash and carrying the short cane. This was a form of drill or marching order. Full dress was worn on normal parade while state dress was worn on parades at which the sovereign was present.

STATE DRUMMER
3RD SCOTS GUARDS

ABOVE: The title of Drum Major has been used in the Foot Guards since the formation of the regiments. A contemporary drawing illustrates a Drum Major of the Coldstream Guards in 1670 and a document dated 1697 gives the Scots Guards Drum Major as receiving the same pay as a sergeant, 1s 6d per diem. In 1881 the title was changed to that of Sergeant Drummer but in 1928 King George gave approval for the original title to be revived. The title on this 1905 post card is not strictly accurate, referring to state dress.

ABOVE: The Scots Guards on manoeuvres. This photograph was taken at Churn camp and appears to have been very hurriedly posed for the photographer but it is interesting in showing that while the corporal and guardsmen present arms the Lance Sergeant carries his rifle at the 'shoulder'. His tunic is of the same quality as the other ranks with white lacing on the cuff flaps and white chevrons. Also of interest is the fact that the 'present' and 'shoulder' as shown was almost identical to that used in the French army during the Napoleonic period. The rifles used by the regiment since 1890 were magazine rifles, the 1890 issue being replaced in 1892 with the Lee-Metford Mark I which in turn was replaced by the Mark II or Long Lee-Metford in 1896.

RIGHT: The Drum Major as he appeared at an annual camp in the late 1890s. The buttons and lacing in groups of threes can be seen in this picture. On the Scots Guards' tunic the bottom button on the lowest group was a dummy or flat button which went beneath the waist belt plate so that only two buttons of the lowest group appeared. On the march at camp the short cane replaced the staff.

The Colours of the 3rd, Battalion, Scots Guards in 1898; the Queen's Colour on the left, the Regimental Colour on the right. The Queen's Colour was crimson and was decorated with the Star of the Order of the Garter and the motto 'Sempur Paratur' (Always ready), the Sphinx badge for Egypt and the regimental battle honours. Above the Garter Star was the Imperial Crown and in the dexter canton a small Union flag. The Regimental Colour is the Union flag with the battalion number in Roman numerals in the dexter canton and the central device is that of the 17th

Company which is the crest of HRH Prince Albert with his motto 'Treu und Fest' (True and fast). The Colours are being held by two Ensigns in Court Guard order and their colour belts have an oblong gilt plate bearing the Star of the Order of the Thistle. In this order of dress the crimson and gold sash was worn and the waist belt and sword slings were gold laced. To the left is the Regimental Sergeant Major with his large Royal Coat of Arms badge on the right arm and to the right is a Battalion Drill Sergeant. The way in which the sword was carried is clearly shown in this picture.

ABOVE: Men of the 1st Battalion, Scots Guards are shown embarking on the Nubia at Southampton at the start of their journey to take part in the South African War. The rank and file all wear their grey greatcoats and either the forage cap or white foreign service helmet, while the small group of officers standing by the near gangway are wearing the blue undress frock. On both sides of the officers' helmet puggaree there is a small patch of regimental diced lace.

OPPOSITE: This interesting montage shows members of the Sergeants Mess in 1897. The Warrant Officers in the front rank wearing peaked caps include Band Sergeants, Quartermaster Sergeants with 4 bar chevrons, Musketry staff and Drill Sergeants. The men in the two rear ranks are all Lance Sergeants, they did not wear the crimson sash and their rank chevrons were white. The chevrons for Sergeants upwards were gold.

The officers of the 1st Battalion, 1896. The officer standing to the left of the group is the Regimental Quartermaster. His uniform was the same as for regimental officers except that his headdress was a cocked hat, black with a loop of 1 in. gold lace and an upright plume 5 in. long made from swans' feathers. His sword belt was of black leather. The officer seated to the Quartermaster's left is the Regimental Medical Officer who also wore the uniform of a regimental officer except that he wore a cocked hat with drooping plume of cocks feathers 6 in. long. His pouch and waist belts were the same as for the Royal Army Medical Corps but with waist plate and pouch device of regimental pattern. Seated in the front row are a General Officer and two Staff officers.

This group showing the officers of the 1st Battalion Scots Guards, was probably taken on the regiment's annual inspection parade shortly before the South African War. The Ensigns are holding the Regimental and Queen's Colours. The Regimental Colour was crimson and bore the Scottish arms, a red lion on a yellow ground with a crown above, the Sphinx, and battle honours scrolls. The Queen's Colour was the Union flag also bearing battle honours but the central device was the badge of one of the companies with the Imperial Crown above and the Sphinx badge below. The officers in the Guards regiments carried their sword with the lower sling attached to the scabbard and hooked up to the waist belt. The exception was Field Officers who always carried their sword on long slings in mounted duty fashion.

A most interesting picture which gives a good idea of everyday life for the 'shilling a day' soldier immortalised in Kipling's famous ballads. Here men of a Scots Guards battalion are seen 'marching easy' during a route march on summer manoeuvres, probably in 1898 or 1899. The bearskin cap was worn, theoretically at least, under active service conditions at home, though the field service cap was also issued. On the left is the battalion signal section, the men carrying rolled up signal flags. They are followed by a mounted orderly and the pipes and drums. The drummers have their drums slung on their backs. Lastly comes a rifle company, rifles at the slope. Many of the men carry their bearskins and wear the FS cap. Note the characteristic drift of dust from the unmetalled road surface and the shape of things to come in the form of a Fowler traction engine which is probably towing a trailer of battalion stores.

The Irish Guards

A Lance Sergeant drummer of the Irish Guards is here decorating the regimental mascot's silver collar with shamrock. This is part of the ceremony which takes place yearly on St Patrick's Day. The shamrock is brought over from Ireland and at the parade a piece is presented to all the officers and men for wearing on the tunic. The drums are also decorated with shamrock. The regimental mascot is always an Irish Wolfhound, the first being 'Brian Boru', presented to the regiment in 1900.

ABOVE: This photograph shows men of the Irish Guards at rifle drill. The white cloth drill jackets worn by three of the men were quite plain with brass buttons of regimental pattern, nine down the front and one on each cuff.

BELOW: A Lance Sergeant drummer and members of the corps of drums, 1904. The fife case suspended from the waist belt can be seen on the left hand figure. The drummer in the centre is wearing the white drill jacket which was discontinued in 1914.

The Regimental Sergeant Major, 1913. The Royal Arms on the right arm as his badge of rank was introduced around 1881. Before this the badge was a smaller Royal Arms superimposed on a 4 bar chevron. The two badges of the regiment can be seen, on the forage cap the regimental badge of the Star of the Order of St Patrick and on the collar the Shamrock. His medals include those for South Africa and for Long Service.

This illustration dates from 1902, showing the Irish Guards Corps of Drums marching past Marble Arch in drill order. They are wearing the plain white drill jacket, a single breasted unadorned garment cut high to the waist. The Broderick caps have a green band, dark blue crown, and carry the regimental badge (Star of the Order of St Patrick). It seems likely that this occasion was a rehearsal for the Coronation parade of King Edward VII for the nearest figure is a sergeant (with slung rifle) who is carrying a rolled-up marker flag. Behind him is a drill sergeant or RSM who appears to be measuring the pace. Note that the normal belt and accoutrements are worn with the drill jacket.

A well-known, but nonetheless interesting picture showing a group of Lieutenants of the Irish Guards in August 1914 at the time of the outbreak of the Great War. Second from right is Lieutenant the Hon P. G. Alexander who later became Earl Alexander of Tunis, one of the greatest of Britain's military leaders in World War 2. The uniform is field service dress, originally introduced in this broad general style in 1908. The tunic is khaki with buttons grouped in fours in the traditional manner. The other Guards regiments followed their own customary groupings on the service tunic. Note the absence of pleats on the pockets and detail differences in the collar styles. The cap band is green and the belts are all in brown leather. Alexander is wearing tan or light whipcord breeches while the others wear khaki trousers or breeches (IWM—Q66199).

August 6, 1914, two days after Britain's declaration of war, and the 1st Bn Irish Guards prepares to march out of Wellington Barracks at 4 o'clock in the morning. The men are wearing Field Service Dress, of khaki serge tunic and trousers dating from 1908. The Pattern 1908 Web, Infantry Equipment is being worn which featured pouches for Lee-Enfield magazine clips. Rounds are being sorted, counted, and stowed away in the foreground. Note the brass 'IG' shoulder titles on the shoulder straps. The cap badge appears to have been dulled on all the caps visible. Brass shoulder titles in abbreviated form were (and still are) worn on shoulder straps by all Guards regiments in service dress (IWM—Q66157).